MW01097421

Devotions for Outdoor Adventures

Devotional Thoughts from and for
Backpackers, Hikers, Climbers,
Canoeists and Other Outdoor
Enthusiasts

Larry Wiggins, Jack Harris
and Amy Garascia

Illustrations by Jack Ballard

Table of Contents

Foreword

Amy, the two Jacks and Larry are dedicated outdoors people. We have been both participants and leaders for groups going into the outdoors for many years. We have worked with Scout age youth, college students and other adults. Our goal has been to teach others how to safely enjoy and learn lessons from the activities that are discussed in this book.

The physical skills involved in outdoor activities are important and are recreational skills that can be used throughout a person's life. However, we consider the opportunity to see God's hand at work in His creation the most important aspect of our outdoor activities. Even Jesus, before he began his active ministry, spent 40 days in the wilderness communing with the Father. Paul, in Romans 1:20 explains why we feel a closeness with God in the outdoors, "For since the creation of the world God's invisible qualities—his eternal power and divine nature—have been clearly seen, being understood from what has been made, so that men are without excuse."

We hope this devotional book will help others see God in the outdoors. We anticipate that this book will be used by individuals in their personal quiet times. Church camps, Scouts and outing clubs can also use the lessons as group devotions while at camp or on outdoor trips. We also hope that the ideas presented will be the basis for further discussion and that the lessons learned in the outdoors will continue to affect the lives of people when they return home to their regular routines.

We would all like to thank George Davis for his effort in reviewing the manuscript.

Mutiny

Scripture: Psalm 121

I planned the trip. I recruited the guys who were there. I made the backcountry reservations. I held training sessions for everyone who had not been in the backcountry before. I rented the canoes and supplied quite a bit of the equipment. I bought and repackaged the food.

The trip was the culmination of my dream to take a group of men canoeing in Canada. I began the work on it months before and planned all the details right down to the condiments that went with the menus.

We canoed for several delightful days under my leadership. Everyone was having a great time enjoying the beauty of the Canadian wilds, being stretched in their abilities and making new friends. It was the first wilderness adventure for several of the men. It was a wonderful experience.

But now, several days out, I was sitting in a campsite and the guys were telling me, "You are not the leader now." Unfortunately, they were right. While cooking dinner, a pan of boiling water was knocked over onto my leg, resulting in a large burn that needed professional attention. My assistant leader took charge and made decisions concerning how the other men would continue the trip and how I would get help. The fact that he was right did not make it any easier for me to give up control. I had worked too hard putting the trip together and I knew how I wanted to handle the situation.

Is that the way we handle our lives? We work so hard keeping everything together. We make so many plans. We have such tight schedules. We have so many places we want to be. In reality, we would be much better off if we turned our lives over to God and let Him in His infinite wisdom be in charge of our plans and schedules.

What areas in your life do you try to control? What decisions are you making on your own? Is it really us who mutiny against God's rightful place as leader of our lives?

Lost

Scripture: Psalm 53

Right from the start I want to tell you that I was not really lost. "Temporarily Spatially Disoriented" or "The Trail Disappeared" just did not seem like catchy titles.

The time was a trip to the Great Smoky Mountains National Park over Christmas break while I was in college. My friend and I drove to the park and camped in his van in a public campground at the bottom of the mountain.

The weather was not all that great, but we had come far enough that we were not going to let a little drizzle stop us from enjoying the trip. So, we took off up the mountain. The details of the trip have become fuzzy over the years, but I seem to remember that the trail went from the bottom of the park to the top of the ridge that goes to Clingmans Dome. Looking back, this seems like a really long day hike, but that is what we were doing. I doubt whether we took any food along with us. Since we were on college time, it is likely that we started late and had no set time when we wanted to be back to the campground.

As we hiked up the mountain, the drizzle changed to snow. It was one of those pretty snows with big fluffy flakes. We did not think much about it at first even though the snow was wet and soaked through our clothes. We kept trekking. As we went up the hill, we noticed that it was harder and harder to find the trail. We got off it once and found it again. Finally we were off the trail and did not know where to find it.

Our next action should have been to take stock of what we had and follow our footprints back to the trail and back down the mountain. What we did, though, was to say that we could not be too far from the road if we went in a certain direction. (Do not ask me what direction that was, since we did not have a compass. We really did not have any safety gear or supplies.) We had looked at the map and knew that if we went downhill we would hit one of the main park roads, eventually.

We did find the road, but not until well after dark and by that time we were soaked to the bone. I can to this day still remember the blue marks my new jeans left in the clean white snow as the dye bled from them as we stumbled down the mountain.

How often in our daily lives do we brazenly go off in our own direction? Often we know that we are not on a path, but we think we can find the trail if we push along farther.

Psalm 53 talks about a fool who says there is no God. When we find our own path and do not depend on God as our compass, are we following a path like a fool?

Are you lost and not admitting it to yourself? Whose directions are you following?

Looking at Nature from the Bottom

Scripture: Matthew 10:29-31, Psalm 139:1-18

My first cave visit was as a boy on a family vacation to Mammoth Cave in Kentucky. In the caverns, grottos and fissures we saw "bottomless" pits, stalactites and stalagmites. These formations were very impressive and I caught an enthusiasm for exploring underground.

Since this trip as a youth, I have explored many caves and have had the opportunity to lead numerous trips to introduce others to the beauty that exists underground in the exquisite details of calcite, gypsum, selenite and other materials. I find joy in discovering both the large formations and the delicate crystals so small that one needs a magnifying glass to clearly see them. I have seen beauty that few others have a chance to see. I have been in corners of caverns that only a handful of other people have explored.

Although I got an early start at caving, it was much later in my life when I discovered the formation I consider most impressive in a noncommercial cave in West Virginia. As we were crawling, walking and climbing through countless passages, I often glanced up to keep from hitting my helmet and head. As I looked up, I discovered that the ceiling of one passage was covered with fossilized shells. There were literally thousands, if not tens of thousands, of these small fossils crowded together. I could not believe what I saw.

Fossils are not formations that you normally think about when you go into caves, and these small fossils were not particularly grand. What impressed me about them was that God knew each of the many creatures there, just as Jesus stated in Matthew, "Yet not one of them falls to the ground apart from your Father's will." All the intricate details that are part of the formations in a cave are expressions of the details of God's creation. He personally takes an interest in each one.

The scripture passage mentions sparrows. They are very common, insignificant birds. Yet, God sees each one of them as significant. If the Father feels that way about the common sparrow, he must have much greater feelings for us as people, created in His image. In Psalms it says, "You carefully observe me when I travel or when I lie down to rest; you are aware of everything I do." God knows us with a true intimacy and truly cares for us. Even in the caves of our own creation, we cannot hide from the love of God. As the Psalmist says, "You knew me thoroughly, my bones were not hidden from you, when I was made in secret, and sewed together in the depths of the earth."

The God of the details in the cave is the same God of the details in my life. He invested in me and knows me better than I know myself.

Have you felt known by God lately?

The Trees of Seneca

Scripture: Psalm 71:1-5

When I climb at Seneca Rocks in West Virginia, I marvel at the trees clinging to the rocks. The roots crawl in and out of every crack and crevice. The trees stand against the wind, rain and snow. They strive and strain and survive. They reach around rocks and boulders literally holding some together.

These trees are the victors in long years of struggle. They find minimal nourishment in crumbling rock and water as it quickly drains after a rain. They find sun when it rises or sets on their side of the mountain. They live in conditions that are not ideal for growing.

Some of the trees are scrawny and bent in odd directions, while others climb to majestic heights. The trees lean at different angles over the sides of cliffs and rocks. In my mind, all of them are miracles.

Many climbers use these trees, clinging perilously to the sides of the cliffs, as anchors. They are used as anchors while belaying others climbing the cracks and as rappel points for descending hundreds of feet.

In recent years I noticed some of my favorite trees died and fell from the mountain. Bolts and chains drilled and hooked deep into the rock for a solid, secure hold have replaced other trees. Still, many climbers continue to trust the trees with their lives and the lives of their companions. They place their faith in these trees that are hugging the mountainside to keep them from falling.

Before the bolts and chains, I also used the trees as anchors. I trusted them and in some locations I still have no choice but to continue trusting them – old, tired, wind-scarred trees.

Do I have such faith in God, who has deeper roots than the trees? Do I believe in the One who created the rocks? Am I wise enough to make the proper decision of what will be long-lasting for my safety? Do I trust One who is stronger, more secure and better anchored than anything in my life? Have I, who have trusted tired trees, trusted God who never tires?

Island Fire

Scripture: Genesis 1:27-31

It was a bright sunny, morning with a cool breeze as Joshua and I canoed the eight kilometers across the choppy, emerald waters of Dickson Lake. We followed the paddling with a long, rough, sweaty five-kilometer portage to Round Island Lake where we collapsed by the shore. It was about 1:00 p.m. as we crawled into the canoe and pushed off from land with a sense of successful exhaustion. We paddled 40 feet from shore, stopped long enough to scoop up and guzzle a quart of fresh water each, and pushed on deeper into the wilderness. We wanted to find a campsite, have lunch and go swimming.

The map showed five campsites on the lake with one on a small island. We headed for the island, looking forward to the end of our day's push. It was a tiny island, fully wooded with trees and bushes right to the water's edge. As we approached it, I saw smoke and wondered what happened since we had seen no one all day and there were no canoes beached there. When we pulled up to shore, we saw the island was on fire.

Previous campers had failed to extinguish their campfire. Something smoldering in the stone ring slipped between the cracks of the rocks and burned through the duff, the ground cover of compressed pine needles, bark, dirt and leaves. The fire evidently had smoldered along for a day or two, consuming a section about 15 feet by 10 feet. The duff was now smoking ash, collapsed 10 to 12 inches below its former level. The edges of the area were still burning as the rough circle pushed farther from the fire ring.

One edge of the fire was just now licking at a tree and starting to char the roots. Another edge was nearing a large pile of dried firewood. Either of these could soon ignite and turn this small fire into a full flare-up. The wind could then spread the sparks to the mainland, which was in the midst of a dry season severe enough that the park was considering a fire ban.

Joshua and I dug into our gear and snatched two small pots to carry water from the shore to dump on the fire. Later we emptied a small dry bag and scooped up larger amounts of water. We soaked the entire burned area and then wet the duff two feet out from the edge. We stopped, had some lunch and drenched it all again, this time, extending our area three feet out. Joshua then used a stick to turn over each area while I dumped more water on anything that looked dry. We estimated we hauled around 300 – 400 gallons to extinguish the fire.

We stayed at a different campsite that night and checked the island site again in the morning before leaving the lake. Later in the day, we ran into a couple going toward the lake and asked them to check the site another time.

One of the things I enjoy about long canoe trips in Canada is the incredible beauty. Yet it would not exist without care. We were fortunate to stop a fire that could mar the beauty that we enjoy. We reported our discovery to the rangers at the end of our trip and were told they lose 10 to 12 campsites a year from careless fires.

God gave us a beautiful world as part of His creation. In Genesis, God gives us stewardship of the earth. It is ours to enjoy, but it is also our responsibility. We need to care for our environment if we want to have it around to enjoy. We need to be careful with fires, trash and waste.

Are you a good steward when you enjoy the wilderness?

Tracks

Scripture: Ephesians 5:6-21, James 2:14-18

The last of the autumn leaves were falling, covering the landscape with a thick, colorful blanket. The backpacking class was hiking in three smaller groups to lessen the impact on the environment. I accompanied the middle crew, about a half-hour behind the first team.

We spent the day leisurely covering the miles with stops to eat and explore. The students learned and enjoyed themselves as we traversed the rolling hills of the Morrison Trail in Allegheny National Forest. We even followed a deer trail and found ripe apples on an old tree that was part of a long-deserted farm.

It was mid-afternoon and we needed to reach our rendezvous point. The route was an older one and sections had been moved through the years to minimize erosion. The students struggled to find blazes to stay on the current trail. We reached a split in the trail where it was unclear which was the main trail and which was the older section. I used my tracking skills and found signs that the first group had taken the left fork. We followed these tracks and 15 minutes later found the group sitting off to the side of the trail waiting for us.

Later, as we set up camp, I pondered the tracking that I did that afternoon. In the dry leaves it was easy for me to distinguish the path the others had taken, although the students could not see it as clearly. I began to wonder what kind of tracks my life leaves for others to follow. Is my trail clear, distinct and something I would want followed, or would I rather conceal my trail and hide it from those behind me? Do I dodge and duck and double back to confuse others or do I mark my way to make it easy for others to see? How does God see us? Do we attempt to cover our tracks from Him and hide like Adam and Eve in the garden or do our tracks clearly show that we walk with Christ?

The Scripture passage in Ephesians speaks of how our deeds become evident when exposed to the light. All of these deeds become tracks that others will see. Our ability to make "good" tracks comes through the gift of the Spirit, who directs our actions.

What kind of tracks are you leaving for others to follow? Where do your tracks lead? Are you trying to hide them? Is God pleased with your trail?

Soar Like Eagles

Scripture: Isaiah 40:28-31

I was tired. We had just finished 12 hours of caving in addition to the long drive to the caving area. The day was spent climbing, squirming, rappelling, crawling and dragging our bodies through a fascinating maze of passages. I felt very fatigued and slightly dehydrated as we walked the last hundred yards to the cave opening. We changed clothes inside where it was warmer, gathered the packs and safety gear we had stashed at the cave mouth and organized the team for the trip back down the mountain.

Since I was the last to crawl out into the crisp February night air, I closed the cave gate behind me. I ducked under the outer lip of the cave entrance, stood up and shouldered my pack to begin the long, laborious hike back to the vans. I moved forward and then stopped. The view from the mountain as we ascended to the cave that morning had been incredible. The path traversed a steep mountainside overlooking a river coursing through a V-shaped valley far below. As I left the cave, I expected there would be no view in the dark, but I was thankfully wrong. The winter air was clear. Stars sparkled in an inky sky over the treetops and the occasional light deep in the valley hundreds of feet below glistened on the snow.

The weariness began to drain from me as I was confronted by a sense of the presence of God. After all, this was the end of a great day. Our caving time was one of safety and a time of fun, exploration, discovery and fellowship. The students were in awe of the cave formations they saw and they were well pleased with their personal response to the challenges and struggles of the day. I sensed how upbeat everyone was and how excited they were about what we accomplished.

Isaiah explains how the Lord gives strength to the weary. Even the young stumble and fall, but those who hope in the Lord will renew their strength. This was happening to me. I was being energized by the beauty of God's creation and His presence in the success of the people around me.

The time spent hiking back to the vans turned not into a time of drudgery but of sharing in the successes of the day—of each person and the entire group. The moment at the front of the cave gave me an eagle's view of God's world and began the process of strengthening me for the balance of the trip.

Are you trusting in God's strength? Can you see the world and your circumstances through His eyes instead of through your own weary perspective?

Get Joel!

Scripture: John 3:16

"Get Joel!" I gurgled when my head broke the chilly surface of the river. When I bobbed up again seconds later, I again shouted, "Get Joel!" Our canoe flipped at the beginning of a 300-yard stretch of white water on the Missinaibi River in northern Ontario, Canada. The first 50 feet of the rapids were a wild class three and the remainder an easier class two. Our canoe hit a "hole" at the beginning of the class three rapids and I failed to brace quickly enough. The canoe rolled and we found ourselves in the fast-moving, rocky water.

We positioned ourselves with the canoe in front of us, pointed our feet downriver and bounced off the unforgiving rocks of the rapids. My attention turned to my teenage son. I immediately started worrying about him as we first came to the surface. True, he was a competent swimmer and knew how to handle himself in white water, but he is my son and my parental concern kicked into high gear.

Other members of our canoe team were stationed along the rocky shore with rescue ropes, but we drifted too far away for them to reach us. Another canoe, stationed two-thirds of the way down the rapids, shot out and scooped up Joel, while the canoe and I continued to bump downriver toward calmer waters.

Once I was past the fast current, I swam the canoe to a shallow area and emptied it. I then waded to the shore, grabbed our dry bags, gathered our other team members and we resumed the day's trip.

To this day when I see the deeply dented side of the canoe I am amazed at the instinctive responses parents demonstrate to protect their children. There is a desire to keep one's son or daughter safe no matter the cost. We put them first and are concerned about their health and well being above our own.

The Scriptures describe God as our Father and makes it clear that He loves us more than our own parents love us. A father's love for a son or daughter is a great phenomenon. God's love for us is greater.

A father's love for a child! God so loved the world that He gave us His Son to die on the cross, though I am sure it conflicted with His own protective instincts. God loves us that much!

Would you as a parent sacrifice your son or daughter for someone else's sin? Does your lifestyle reflect the sacrifice God made for you?

Teach Me Your Paths

Scripture: Psalm 25:4-5, 32:8

Six freshman students, another leader and I huddled in the rain. We watched the car and the van with the second group of students pull out of the parking lot by Dry Fork River. It was not dry. After they dropped us off, the other group headed for the Dolly Sods for the Labor Day weekend and they would pick us up on Monday afternoon at the other end of our trail.

It was past midnight. We shouldered our packs in the constant drizzle and stepped onto a bridge to begin our hike into the Otter Creek Wilderness Area in West Virginia. The suspension bridge swayed under the cadence of the eight of us as we tried not to slip on the wet surface. After the bridge, we were hemmed in by a rock wall on our left and the gushing creek on our right. This created additional moments of anxiety for several students as we slowly worked our way along the narrow path of slick rocks. The sound of the rushing water vibrated through the ground and into our booted feet, reminding us that a slip would be very dangerous.

We stopped frequently to adjust packs and replace batteries in lights that had not used recently. The inability to clearly see the trail in the mist with our weak lights only added to the risk and confusion. We adjusted clothing to remain dry in the persistent spitting of the rain. There was a hush within the group as we threaded our way around the nighttime obstacles of slippery mud, logs and stones with the continual roar of Otter Creek beside us. I could almost hear a collective sigh of relief when we finally reached a wider, leveler path with more space on each side.

We only trudged a mile through the mud and wet scrubs that night before we found an area that would serve as a campsite. The weary students dropped their packs and began the process of learning how to erect tents, put up tarps and sort gear, all in the rainy darkness.

It was one week into the new college year and this was a group of freshmen on a three-day trip, learning the basics of backpacking. We taught them not only the ways of the woods, but also the ways of God. One purpose of the trip was to consider how God would direct them in the coming years of college.

One student later shared Psalm 25 with us and explained that she was aware of God guiding her during our anxious entrance into Otter Creek. As a result, she felt that He was telling her that He would teach her and lead her not only through her years of college but throughout her life. She completed her college years under His guidance and recently finished seminary in preparation for mission work.

Is God showing you His ways and paths for your life? Are you listening for his direction?

Mountaintop Experience

Scripture: Psalm 150

Eighteen years is a long time, a very long time. But that is how much time passed from when I first saw Mt. Rainier from a plane to my successful summit of the mountain's volcanic peak.

My summit attempt began on Tuesday when we spent the day learning how to use our ice axes, crampons, mountaineering boots and other equipment. We learned how to stop and go while traversing the steep inclines of the mountain, how to work as a member of a roped team and how to arrest a slide down a snowy, icy slope. It was a great day of training and getting to know our teammates.

We spent Wednesday hiking up the almost four miles and 5,000 vertical feet from Paradise to where Camp Muir is perched on a ridge high above the valley. We trudged through the snowfields in shorts and sweat-soaked T-shirts with full packs under the hot, late July sun. We used our ski poles for balance, practiced our rest step and thought about our breathing pattern. We started developing the rhythm we would need for climbing to the top.

On Thursday, we left Camp Muir just before 1:00 a.m. We swallowed some breakfast and spent 45 minutes arranging our gear and packs one last time. Our crampons were on our boots and our ice axes were snugly held in our gloved hands. We checked our supply of food and water, clipped into the rope behind our guide, stepped onto Cowlitz Glacier and began the seven-plus hour trip up the Disappointment Cleaver route to the top of the 14,410-foot volcano.

It was cool when we started and became colder as the icy

air rolled down the glaciers and snow fields over us. As long as we kept moving we were warm. When we stopped for a break, my down mountaineering coat was a necessity. The air thinned as we got higher and the breathing practice of the previous days became essential as we gained altitude. We successfully made it to the summit, rested and began the trip back to Camp Muir and then down to Paradise by late in the day.

Climbing Mt. Rainier was the completion of an 18-year goal, but the most important part of the trip happened earlier. Shortly after midnight I stepped out of the RMI hut at Camp Muir just prior to our final push to the top. I will always remember that moment. I have seen many beautiful, star-studded skies in the course of leading wilderness trips in the United States and Canada. I have enjoyed watching the aurora borealis. But this was different. We were at 10,000 feet, above the valley haze, more than 100 miles from any major city and there had been no clouds for days. It was the most incredible sky, full of countless stars, more than I have ever seen before. I started worshiping God and humming "How Great Thou Art" about seeing His stars and His power throughout the universe. Others also noticed the stars, but I felt the presence of the Holy Spirit. I waited 18 years to climb Mt. Rainier and it climaxed with opportunity to worship God. It was an amazing experience.

What leads you into God's presence? Have you had an unanticipated time of worship lately?

Wind

Scripture: Romans 7:14-25

When paddling a canoe, the wind is a major issue. No matter which direction you are traveling, the wind seems to be blowing against you. On a two-week Canadian river trip, we had a strong wind in our face for two days. When we stopped paddling, the wind blew us upriver against the current. The second day we were forced to pull over to the bank to wait until evening when the wind calmed.

I had another experience with the wind on a week-long trip with my Boy Scout troop. Earlier during the week, we taught tandem paddling techniques and on our last day we covered solo paddling. Solo paddling is difficult for beginners, especially that day since the wind had picked up. We were on a large lake where there was little shelter, but we did find some relief in the lee of a peninsula. As long as we stayed behind the peninsula, the water was relatively calm for our training session.

I usually make it a practice of not working with my sons on skills like this because I become impatient with them. On this occasion, my son was the last Scout to go out and I teamed with him. As we began, it seemed that he did the opposite of everything I told him to do. When I told him to paddle forward, he paddled backward. When I told him to kneel in the bottom of the canoe, he sat in the bottom.

As we worked, I could not get Matt to paddle away from the wind. Our canoes were drifting out of the shelter of the peninsula into the main lake and an even stronger wind than when we started. The wind caught us and sent us flying across the lake. In the end, it was necessary for another canoe with two leaders to rescue my son. They chased after him, caught his canoe, tied a rope to it and pulled him back to calm water.

Is this the way our lives go? When God wants us to do one thing, we do something else. If we are to be in one position, we are usually in another. Like Jonah, we run in the opposite direction of where we are told to go. Paul speaks of doing what he ought not to do and not doing what he ought to do. We often travel contrary to God's intentions, heading straight into the wind, instead of following His leading and traveling with His guiding wind at our backs.

Are you fighting the wind on your own or are you traveling with God's leading?

Heavenly Provisions

Scripture: Psalm 84:11, 1 Corinthians 2:9, Ephesians 3:20

I love to go backpacking. I enjoy each stage of the trip: planning, packing, hiking (especially if the terrain is flat or only moderately steep) and camping in pristine areas. There is nothing like falling asleep to the sound of a stream or waking up on a sunny morning to fresh air, nature and good company. Even better is a crisp fall day with dried leaves crunching underfoot.

But my absolute favorite aspect of backpacking is cooking. I will skimp on everything in my pack so that I can carry my stove that will simmer, my oven and a fuel bottle. I love to cook at home. But outside, in my camp chair, is my favorite place to cook. I sit surrounded by foodstuffs, pans, cooking utensils, a mug filled with a hot drink, a sharpened knife, a hot stove and a headlamp. With everything in reach, I begin to make a meal.

Have you ever noticed how everything tastes better when you are camping? Even macaroni and cheese is delicious. But I like to go a step further and bake a dessert or make a soup or casserole with fresh vegetables. My favorite food to bake is really quite simple. It involves the ingredients for pizza dough, with a few extras like olive oil, onions, spices and Parmesan cheese. Let it rise, then let it bake and you have the most delicious focaccia bread. As a matter of fact, I only make focaccia bread when I am camping because it does not taste as good when I make it at home.

We can think of God's provision for our lives in a similar way. He wants to provide the basic necessities for us. But He also wants to go above and beyond, for He "is able to do immeasurably more than all we ask or imagine, according to his power that is at work within us". He will give us the macaroni and cheese, but He really desires for us to have the focaccia bread.

It is easy to have faith when things are going well and God's provision is evident. But when you are seeking direction and are not sure which way to go, it is harder to trust Him.

Are you trusting Him to provide for you and meet your daily needs? Are you expecting macaroni and cheese or focaccia bread?

Moonlight

Scripture: Ephesians 5:6-14

One very vivid memory I have of Fiji is the full moon. The moon there seemed to be brighter than anywhere I have ever been. I can remember wanting to try to read a book by moonlight. On the full-moon nights I was often lured to hike along the beach. I would start after dinner and hike around a point near where I lived just to enjoy the moonlight. I never measured the distance, but I probably covered 10 miles in an evening.

I know that there are other places where the night sky can be that clear and enjoyable. In the mountains where the air is thin, the night sky is especially brilliant. When you are away from the "light" pollution of the cities, the moon and multitudes of stars are even crisper.

Jesus said that we are "the light of the world." As Christians our light is very much like moonlight. The moon has no light source of its own. It can only reflect the light of the sun. We also cannot emit light on our own. We must reflect the light of the Son of God.

Many people are very familiar with this analogy. What we should think about is what kind of pollution is blocking the light that is reflecting from us. Is there a source of light pollution that dims our light? Is there haze in the air that takes away the crispness of our light? Are there clouds that completely block our light?

In Ephesians there are references to both the darkness caused by sin and the light of Jesus, which reveals everything about our lives. Sin in our lives dims or even completely blocks the light that we reflect. If we represent ourselves as Christians, then every time we fall short of what we know God wants us to do, our light is dimmed. Our goal should be to reflect the brilliant light as if we are in a clean tropical setting or the thin atmosphere of the mountain.

How much light are you reflecting? What keeps you from reflecting all of the Son light?

Storms

Scripture: Hebrews 12:1-3

We pitched camp on a very picturesque point on Lake Louisa in Algonquin Provincial Park in Ontario, Canada. This point sits with the main lake to the north and cliffs on a large bay to the west. An attraction of this site was that the water under the cliffs was deep enough for jumping. The location of the campsite provided views of the lake and, hopefully, beautiful sunsets. We even had two nights to enjoy our location.

Unfortunately as we finished setting up our tents, we saw a storm approaching from the west. As I checked the camp one last time, the storm arrived and the wind tossed one of our ultra-light canoes 20 feet into the lake.

The canoe was quickly blowing away, so I launched another canoe and started after the one fleeing with the wind. By this time the rain was coming down in sheets. What really startled me, though, as I approached the canoe on the lake was that the wind suddenly stopped and the lake surface was very smooth, except for the impact of the rain. This calm period allowed me to catch up to the drifting canoe and tie a line to it. Almost immediately the wind resumed its ferocity and I had to fight to pull the canoe back to shore.

Consider the passage in Hebrews where we are called to persevere. There are times in our lives when in spite of the storms around us, we may have a calm as I observed on the lake that afternoon. The peace that we obtain through God calming either our circumstances or ourselves allows us to continue the "race that is set before us." It would not have helped when I noticed the lake was smooth to sit there and enjoy the view. I needed to retrieve the canoe and get it back to shore.

Just one month and one day from the storm on Lake Louisa, I experienced a more severe storm. I was in the radiology department of a hospital where I was told that my son had a tumor that would be removed as soon as he could be scheduled for surgery. The storm of not understanding his prognosis and the ensuing treatment was devastating. The surgery revealed cancer and the storm continued through nine weeks of chemotherapy.

During this process I was scared, angry and discouraged. But fortunately I had the hope and the peace that comes from knowing that God is in control. God gave our whole family the peace and the endurance to survive the ordeal. Today, as I write this almost six months after his diagnosis, my son has resumed his education and is continuing his life. His prognosis is good and I continue to pray for his complete healing.

All of us experience storms in our lives. They may be small ones that pass quickly and we barely notice them or they may be crises like severe health problems.

What kind of storms are you experiencing? When these storms arrive do you trust God and continue in the work that He asks even while the storm continues to rage around you?

Lightweight Backpacking

Scripture: Philippians 3:12-16

When you select your gear for backpacking, weight is a major consideration. You repackage food to cut down on excess wrapping and weight. You may choose freeze-dried foods, not because you like the taste, but because they weigh so much less than other foods. Your tent probably is a tight fit for the number of people that will be sharing it. If you think the weather and the bugs might be favorable, you might forgo your tent for a lightweight tarp. Some people even shorten the handle on their toothbrush to save weight and carry only a cup and spoon for eating purposes.

You look for lightweight, layerable clothing, lightweight boots and lightweight packs. You select your clothes to be functional, but also multipurpose so you can make do with fewer items. You may carry a lighter sleeping bag and wear more clothing when you sleep at night to keep warm.

The catalogs and stores are full of many items that are high tech and weigh less. Good catalogs include the weight of each item as part of the description. The ultimate in lightweight gear is the expensive titanium cooking sets which will help you shave ounces from your load.

The reason for this passion to reduce weight is so your backpack and equipment do not weigh you down. With less weight, you can cover more distance; it allows you to travel faster and not be as tired when you arrive at your destination. You can see and do more on your hike.

In Philippians, Paul tells us to get rid of that excess weight and strive toward our goal of life with Christ. If we purchase the right equipment and make do with less when we hike, should we not also make the same effort in our spiritual lives? We should pursue our goal to be more Christlike with more enthusiasm than the backpacker who cuts off his toothbrush handle to save weight.

What do you need to do to lighten your walk with Christ and become more Christlike?

Ice

Scripture: Proverbs 3:1-6, 7:1-3, Deuteronomy 6:4-6

It was a classic winter day. The sun peeked occasionally from behind the clouds. The air was cold and clear with temperatures in the upper teens. Occasionally light snow flurries fell, adding to the beauty of the many inches of snow already on the ground.

It was our second day at Leesville Lake and we were enjoying the bracing air and solitude of a winter camping trip. The lake had been frozen for weeks in the unusually cold year and the wind kept it swept clean of snow. Brian and I were bundled up and quite warm as we crunched out of the snow-encrusted woods onto the ice. We slowed down to test the slipperiness of the ice and then began to cross the lake at a narrow point. We could see the thickness of the ice through deep re-frozen cracks that zigzagged across the surface.

We were halfway across when we heard a loud crack like a gunshot. I dropped immediately onto my stomach with my arms and legs spread out. Brian looked down at me with concern for the sound we just heard and in wonder at the "crazy" person now lying on the lake ice beside him.

From years of reading and some experience with lakes and streams I understood that if you lie down and spread your weight out on ice that is cracking you can keep from breaking through to the cold water below. With care you can safely slide your way to the shore. When I heard the crack of the ice I instinctively responded without giving conscious thought to my actions – I quickly spread my weight out on the lake surface.

If we spend time in the Scriptures reading and mediating

on God's word and spend time in prayer and talking to God we prepare ourselves in much the same way for life. We learn how God would have us act in different circumstances. We will accumulate experience in responding to God's urging in our lives.

As a result, when a crisis or something unexpected happens in our lives we will behave in much the same way I did on that winter day with Brian. We instinctively respond without much thought, to do as God will have us do. Preparation can make a difference in our lives and safety in the wilderness. Time spent with God will prepare us for the greater issues of life. I know I need to spend more time preparing for such predicaments.

How about you? How much time have you spent today in the preparation of prayer and reading God's word?

The Chock

Scripture: Matthew 18:12-14, Matthew 7:9-11

The chock popped out. It had been wedged in by a short lead fall and my son, Joshua, struggled to get it loose. Finally the rocks lost their grip on the chock and it went flying in an arch through the air, landing on a ledge 70 feet below. At the same time, my son lost his balance, tumbling off the face of the cliff after the chock.

As he fell head over heels waiting for the next piece of protection to stop him, he wildly grabbed a stationary rope and received a rope burn from the friction of the rope sliding through his hand. When he came to a sudden stop, his first concern was to let me know that he was OK by shouting that he was "all right." It was another several minutes before he told me about the nasty burn.

Joshua carefully climbed down to me with one hand, removing all but the top chock as I lowered him. Another group arrived at the ledge and they slid our last chock down their rope to us as they climbed the next pitch. We then began the slow, careful process of setting up a rappel and getting to the base of the rocks without doing any further damage to Joshua's hand.

We succeeded in our descent, hiked back to the van and cleaned and bandaged the injured hand. The next day we went hiking instead of the intended climb.

Joshua was wise in calling out to me that he was "all right." He knew that as his father my greatest concern would be for him. Everything else would be secondary, the flying chock, other people on the rocks, even my own safety. Joshua knew my love and concern for him would be a priority because God models that love for us. God created us and loves us more than anything else. He is grieved when we hurt.

What do you love? Do you know how much God loves you? Does your life reflect that you are His priority, His precious child? Is God a priority in your life?

Finding the Way

Scripture: Numbers 14:20-23

Dan had a problem navigating Cache Lake. He admitted that he had never been able to canoe around the various islands and bays and navigate a direct route to the outlet. On his last trip, I rubbed it in by hanging back as he started across the lake. I took the correct route and had a 20 minute nap while Dan canoed the long way.

As we approached Cache Lake on the next trip, everyone knew the stories about how difficult it is to find your way on the lake. They started looking at the map and talking about the difficult navigation, even though Dan was not along on the trip. One of the group members asked if he could canoe with me that day to avoid getting lost. Other members of the party came up with another solution; they would follow me since I did not have the same problem navigating the lake.

When we arrived on the lake, I held back as the group started across the lake. Sure enough, they went down the wrong bay. I did not follow but took the more direct (correct) route. A couple of the canoes only went a few hundred yards before they realized that I was not following them and they turned back. However, the rest of the group followed the lead canoe the wrong way.

Getting lost, in most cases, is an option. Maps, compasses, GPS devices, written and verbal directions are usually available to us. We may choose to not learn how to use these tools, be inattentive to them or to ignore their directions. These are choices that we make either directly or by omission. Any one of these choices could get us lost.

As much as I would like to think so, Dan is not the only

one who gets lost. People have experienced the frustration of not finding their way for thousands of years. Probably the best example of getting lost is the Israelites wandering in the wilderness. Again, getting lost was an option. The Israelites had something even better than satellite navigation. They had God going before them in a cloud by day and fire by night. How then did they manage to get lost for 40 years? They were lost for the same reason most of us are lost. They chose to go their own way in spite of the presence of God.

Most of the time, we do not have such concrete signs from God. But, we are the same as those ancient peoples. We choose to ignore the signs (directions) that we do have. We choose to sin when we know the direction we should take. As people who know the outdoors we should use the lessons we have learned about navigation in the rest of our lives. In place of maps and compasses we have the Bible and prayer. We cannot hope to avoid getting lost in sin without using these tools.

Are you truly following God's way for your life?

Blazes

Scripture: Psalm 119:97-105

My sons and I decided to go backpacking over their Christmas break. We planned to be gone a couple days so we decided to hike the Minister Creek Trail in Allegheny National Forest.

The trip started out beautifully. It was a cold winter day with a few inches of snow on the ground. The trail was easy to follow with its white blazes and someone had been through since the last snowfall so we were able to follow their footprints as well.

We made it to the end of the valley that afternoon and set up camp. There was no one else in the area. It was a great time to be out in the woods!

In the morning the snow started to fall again. It was a fluffy wet snow that stuck to everything and made the setting even more beautiful. We spent the time exploring the area around the campsite and met a ranger and a couple of hunters.

Late in the afternoon, we decided we would hike back out. The snow had accumulated to four inches deep as we started back, covering the footprints of the previous hikers, but we still had the blazes to follow. As we hiked out, we discovered that the white blazes blended in well with the new snow, especially as it stuck to the trees.

We inevitably found that we were off the trail and were not sure when we had seen the last blaze. Since the terrain was simple, we just had to follow the valley back to the car, and since we had a topographical map of the area, traveling off the trail was not a serious concern. The way home was obvious, although my youngest son was greatly concerned about not knowing our exact location.

Is life much the same as this trip? We may follow our chosen trail along easily for a time, without much thought or concern about it. Eventually, our trail will become blurred; the blazes by which we are navigating will blend in with the world around us.

The Psalmist says, "Thy word is a lamp unto my feet and a light unto my path." If we know and study the Bible, which is our map, the terrain becomes discernible and our proper path is revealed.

At the same time there are those around us, like my son, who do not understand the map and the information that it gives. Without that understanding, they cannot trust it or have the assurance that they will not get lost. It is our job to share the map and help them develop their way.

What blazes are you following? What will you do if you find yourself off the trail?

God's Eye View

Scripture: Romans 8:35-39

I clasped another rock, checked my position and stepped higher on the cliff face. I made sure I felt secure and then began juggling chocks as I prepared to place the next one in the rocks. I clipped in my rope and took a moment to look around me before I moved up the cliff.

With each step upward, the valley opened below me. I was now looking at the tops of tall trees that we had walked under a short while ago. Clinging onto the side of a rock and seeing the trees as miniatures gave me an unusual perspective of the world.

As my partner and I climbed higher, we watched birds flying by level with us. Local vultures were soaring on the thermals at eye level. At the next higher pitch, we saw birds launch into the air below us, glide and land elsewhere beneath where we were sitting. It was strange to see the backs of birds in flight. It was so different from our normal view of looking up at them.

Late in the afternoon as we sat near the summit, a small jet plane zoomed up the valley flying close to the rocks below us. It was a bizarre sensation to watch the top of a plane fly by as we sat on a ledge. I had no previous life experience to compare with this one.

To look down on trees from above, to watch the birds' backs in flight, and to be higher than a jet plane is to have a God's eye view of the world. It is a different perspective of the planet than I know. I experienced a glimpse of what our globe and our activities might look like to God as He watches us from above. It gives a broader perspective to the actions that we think are critical and important. God has a different view of our world that could make us meaningless, yet He values us above all else.

Have you considered how you look to God? Are your actions and activities important in His perspective?

Rappel in the Dark

Scripture: Matthew 11:25-30

We take the boys in our Scout troop caving periodically. It is a great trip for them. There is the adventure of exploring the cave and, most importantly, there are the challenges that the boys must face. These include the darkness, tight spaces, cold temperatures and heights. The wonderful thing about the caving experience is that the challenges the Scouts face can be selected and, therefore, they are controlled. As a result of controlling the challenges at a level the boys are able to accomplish, we create a successful experience for them.

Perhaps the biggest challenge for some of the boys is the100-foot rappel between the first and second levels of the cave. On one trip, a boy expressed his concern for this activity early in our planning for the trip. During the preparation the leaders did all they could to reassure him about the safety of the rappel. We instructed him about the strength of the rope, how slow and under control his descent would be and that as a final safety measure, someone would be belaying him who would be able to stop his descent if anything unexpected happened. All of this made sense to the leaders but it really did not reassure the young man.

Knowing how the Scout felt about the situation, I was still concerned for him as we started the rappel. The last help available was the trip leader at the top of the rappel. His experience and teaching ability would get the boy down if anything could. The Scout did make it down the rappel, but it was not easy. To reassure him, the leader rappelled down the cliff on another rope beside the boy and talked him through each step of the decent. This partnership encouraged the boy through the rappel. The Scout had a real sense of accomplishment when he arrived at the bottom.

Jesus made a promise to assist us through rappels that trouble us in our lives. The imagery of being yoked with Jesus is not unlike the leader sharing the rappel experience with the boy in our Scout troop. In the Scripture, Jesus tells us to take his yoke which is easy to bear. Things which we could not do alone we can accomplish together with Christ.

Are you yoked with Christ today in all areas of your life?

The Map

Scripture: Psalm 119:97-106

It was a sunny, Sunday afternoon. A friend and I decided to go hiking after church so we ate lunch, changed clothes and drove to a nearby national forest. By the time we reached the trailhead, it was almost 3:00 p.m.

The friend I was hiking with grew up in the area and usually teased me about carrying a map. I had hiked in the area before and felt relatively comfortable with the area, so I left the map in the car. I assumed my friend knew the trail we would be taking.

We set off along a steep ridge and enjoyed the beautiful views. We stopped for a drink of water, looked at the foliage and the fallen leaves and then hiked further. As we chatted, I realized that my friend had never hiked this particular trail before. I remembered that a number of trails in the area are loop trails, but some are not. I had visions of the trail ending at the local ranger station which would be closed and miles away from the car. I continued to watch the time creep later as we hiked. I determined that if we had not intersected another trail by 4:30, we would turn around and go back the way we came to reach the trailhead by about 6:00 when it would be dark.

At 4:30 we found an intersection, turned off the old trail and headed downhill. I was very glad to be headed in a direction closer to where we wanted to be, but I still did not know where we were. As we crossed a marshy area in the valley, there were a number of trail intersections. We munched on cookies and I wished for the map and a compass and a variety of other outdoor gear that I left behind. We guessed at the direction and continued hiking. We crossed a stream several times and I desperately tried to remember the area from my previous visits. It was dusk when I finally recognized the area. It continued to grow darker as we climbed the last slope to the trailhead, reaching the car as it became dark.

After that trip, I promised myself that I would learn from my mistake and be prepared on future trips. I now regularly carry a water bottle, map and a compass as well as a snack and other supplies. I decided that it is better to be prepared than to depend on someone else to guide me.

In Psalm 119, the Psalmist exalts God's word as a guide for our lives. Just as a map needs to be consulted, so we must read the Bible and live out its truth in our lives.

Are you learning from your past mistakes? Are you prepared for life by reading and meditating upon the Scriptures, God's map for your life?

Rocks

Scripture: Psalm 46

Rocks are everywhere! I dig them out of the flowerbeds. I skied over one this weekend and it caused me to fall. They crack windshields, damage lawn mowers, become weapons for children and are generally a nuisance. Rocks can be real obstacles to avoid.

I also look for rocks. When rocks obstruct flowing water they create the white water that provides a thrill for canoeing. Part of this excitement is knowing that hitting a rock might cause me to take an unplanned swim or damage the canoe.

I love the challenge of navigating through the barriers and blockades that rocks create in the river. With every rise and fall of the water level you are faced with a totally new set of conditions to overcome from the rocks twisting and turning the water in different directions. The unmoving character of the stationary rocks is at odds with the power and force of the moving water.

Navigating white water would be more difficult if I did not know that on the downstream side of the rock is an eddy. An eddy is a quiet spot, protected from the rest of the rapids. The eddy is where you take a break from the torrent and plan your next moves. An eddy is a place of peace where one can rest. It is created by a rock that will not let the water have its way rushing down the river.

I have a friend who, while learning to canoe on a river, found himself in an eddy behind a small rock with four feet of white water rushing by on either side. He marveled at his success in getting into the eddy without being swept past, but was more amazed at sitting in calm, flat water in the midst of the chaos that surrounded him. He experienced the strength and power of a rock.

In Psalm 46, God is described as a secure shelter. In other translations this shelter is described as a rock. God is the eddy where we can seek refuge. When the rapids in our lives are boiling around us and we are out of control, we can duck into God's eddy and find peace. Finding that peace, we can scout ahead and consult with God to help us plot our course through the next stretch of rough water, knowing that God will continue to provide places of refuge whenever we need them.

Are the rocks in your life a hindrance or a help? Are you depending on God to be your Rock and provide eddies of shelter for you in the white water of life?

Bears

Scripture: John 10:22-30, 2 Timothy 4:15-18

My brother was moving from Tennessee to Washington State. Since he would be so far away, we decided to take one last backpacking trip together before he left.

The trip started out well. It was mid-December in the Smoky Mountains and there was some snow left on the ground from a recent snowfall, but this Saturday was warm, delightful and sunny. We hiked to a campground just off the Appalachian Trail near Gregory Bald.

After dinner that evening we hiked up to the bald. The view was spectacular. The night was bright enough that we did not need to use lights to make the short trip to the top.

Shortly after returning to the camp, I went into my tent, while my brother and a friend stayed up talking. Not much later, I heard a commotion outside. From the noise my brother was making, I guessed that there was a bear raiding our food cache.

I pulled on my clothes and left the tent to see what was happening. Sure enough, a black bear was up a tree pulling our bear bag down so he could get to the food. The bear knew what he was doing and he was not going to let us chase him away from the food. After watching the bear eat our food for a while, I went back to the tent. The last thing I remember before falling asleep was hearing the bear walk by the side of the tent only a foot or two from my head.

The ability to go to sleep with a bear that close in a campsite is the kind of trust that Jesus talked about in

John. Jesus holds us in His hand and no one can take us away from Him. We need to be able to ignore the evil and trouble that is around us and go on with what He calls us to be doing.

At the same time, as Paul describes in 2 Timothy, we need to know that we will have problems. We can be assured of the ultimate victory, but that does not mean that we will not encounter bears along the path.

An interesting note is that when we hiked out, hungry the next morning along the same path we had walked in the dark, we saw signs that the bear had been on the path the previous night, probably about the time we were. It is reassuring to know that my Savior is greater than any bear that I may stumble upon in the dark.

What are the "bears" you are encountering in your life? How is God helping you to overcome these obstacles? Do you have faith to trust God in spite of these bears?

Following the Directions

Scripture: Proverbs 3:5-6, 16:9, Psalm 18:30-32

I received a GPS as a Christmas gift last year. The GPS allows you to input your destination, then it calculates directions to reach the destination. This is exactly what the Bible does for us. Our goal is to become more like Christ and share Him with a lost world. The Bible provides us the steps that God uses to mold our character and the guidance to reach out to others.

The first destination that I entered into my GPS was a route that I had traveled numerous times before. I was surprised when the directions were not for my normal route. I had an almost verbal debate about whether to follow the directions for a route that I had never used before or to go the way I normally traveled. What if the directions were wrong? What if they were right and it really was a more direct route? Should I stay with the route that I was familiar with anyway?

In the end, I decided to follow the directions on the GPS. After following the directions, I concluded that it knew the best route better than I did. The new route traversed an area I never traveled before and was, therefore, completely unfamiliar to me. That argument over control perfectly typifies my relationship with God: I can follow the path that I am familiar with or I can release my control and my will and let Him lead. This new territory may be unfamiliar and I will not know the way on my own.

God is the ultimate GPS and He promises to never lead us astray. He does not promise that we will know where we are going (Abram set out for a foreign country without directions), but God promises to be with us and guide us along the way. We just need to be in tune with Him and follow each step of the directions, in the exact order and time given.

Are you following God's directions or trusting in your own understanding?

Portaging

Scripture: 2 Corinthians 4:7-18

Portaging is the process of carrying a canoe and all of your gear from one body of water to another. Portages connect lakes and they bypass obstacles on rivers.

The amount of work to accomplished during a portage varies considerably. Canoes weigh from 40 to 80 pounds. Packs can weigh 25, 50, 70 pounds or even more. The portage trails can be short, flat and easy or they can be steep, muddy and long. Carrying as much as possible on each trip reduces the number of round trips to get everything through the portage. This can necessitate carrying weights from 70 to 100 pounds a trip.

In a video about a Missinaibi River trip in Canada, John Viehman, asked Steve Landick what was the longest portage he had ever taken. Steve's reply was 68 miles. That sounds more like a backpacking trip to me than a portage!

In spite of the difficulties in portaging, I enjoy them. I find that a portage is a good break from paddling and I think that each one gets me farther from civilized areas. At the end of the portage there is a chance to explore new territory, a new segment of nature.

Maybe portaging is like the hardships that Paul describes in 2 Corinthians. We must persevere through the portages of life, not because we enjoy the hardships, but because we appreciate the reward at the end of the trail. Because we are not looking at what can be seen but at what cannot be seen; for what can be seen is temporary, but what cannot be seen is eternal.

When I hoist a canoe to begin a new portage, I know that a beautiful lake or that great white water rapid may be just past the end of the portage. As wonderful as that expectation is, it does not compare to the glory I look for in heaven.

Are you facing any portages in your life? Are you looking forward to the reward at the end of these portages? Are you in the habit of looking beyond the portage to the One who is in charge of your trip?

Washed Away

Scripture: Matthew 7:21-27

One of the tasks that I liked best about my Peace Corps assignment in Fiji was the opportunity to visit villages throughout the region. Many of them were past the end of the road, in the "bush." On one occasion, I took the bus to the end of the line and started hiking up a valley to visit two villages. The farthest village was about five miles away, along a pleasant stream where I had swum and rafted on previous trips.

There was a steady rain when I left the bus, but with the warm temperatures of Fiji, I was not concerned about getting wet. A short distance up the valley a villager offered me the use of a horse for the day. He asked only that I tether it in the same general area when I returned later in the day. I gladly accepted the offer and proceeded on my trip. I spent the day meeting with the people in the villages and I planned my return to catch the last bus in the afternoon.

On my return trip, as I traveled back down the valley and crossed the many fords along the path, I barely noticed the continuous rain had caused the stream to rise. Crossing was not a problem for the horse I was riding with its long legs and strength.

I returned to the spot where I decided to leave the horse, just before the last ford. I tethered the horse and continued on foot. As I waded into the final stream crossing, I was surprised at how high the water had risen. As I entered the current, I was swept off my feet and washed downstream. After traveling about 30 yards I was able to swim to the far shore. This unexpected swim, while exciting, fortunately was not extremely dangerous since there were no hazards in the stream to worry about. I still wonder why I did not just tether the horse on the other side of this last ford.

I experienced a feeling of desperate helplessness as I was swept from my feet and down the stream. This example is really insignificant compared to what Jesus was talking about in the Scripture passage. Without the foundation of the Bible we can be swept away in the currents that are flowing all around us. There are so many things happening in our lives that can sweep us off our feet. What we learn and practice from the Word of God can be our rock. Scripture can be just like my horse that day, helping us to safely wade through the currents of life that seek to sweep us off our feet.

Take some time to think about the many things swirling about your feet. Are your feet firmly placed with God and the Scripture so that you have a foundation when the swirling waters are at their worst?

Help

Scripture John 10:1-18, Psalm 107:1-7

"Jack?! Help!" I was immediately wide awake.

I was leading a group of college students on their first backpacking trip. We covered the planned distanced on a beautiful sunny day and found a flat spot away from the trail for a camp site. The leaders cooked a dessert buffet to follow the students' first personally cooked camp meal (some of their food looked a bit strange). The evening ended with a time of fun, games, stories and discussion around a campfire in a fire pan. It had been a great first day.

There was no moon in the dark sky, but the stars shined like jewels as the students prepared for the night. Since I am a "mother-hen" type, I was one of the last to go to bed. I was lying in my sleeping bag under a tarp listening to the remaining few students adjust gear and bed down. I heard Tammy go up the hill to the bathroom area about 10 minutes earlier. Everything was quiet in the dark and I was between being awake and asleep when I heard her call for help. She missed the camp on her return and was now below us on the hill, realizing she was lost.

I sat up in my sleeping bag, faced the direction of her voice and called to her. She called back and I continued to speak to her in a calm, reassuring voice to guide her toward camp. Eventually I saw her weak light as she struggled up the hill toward me. As she neared the camp, her voice was calmer and less frightened. When she re-entered our camping area and reached the sleeping area with the other students, she was more composed and relaxed.

I sometimes think about that night. It reminds me of the

times God has answered my shout for help in a calm, reassuring voice. I found that He is always alert and always listening for us. He will guide us back to His camp where we are safe. John talks about Jesus being the "Good Shepherd." His sheep know His voice and follow Him. I hope that I am as attentive to His voice as Tammy was to mine that night.

Whose voice are you listening to? Are you lost and searching? Have you called out to God for guidance? Are you following His reassuring words?

Canoe

Scripture: Philippians 1:18-26

I bought my canoe in 1972. At that time there were relatively few choices in canoes. I bought a lightweight aluminum canoe. This boat has carried me many miles, both around lakes in Ohio and on longer trips in Canada. Best of all, it has survived in fairly good condition.

If I were buying a canoe today, the choice would be much more difficult. Do I want a hull designed for white water or one designed to track straight on lakes? Do I want one constructed of a lightweight material for an easy time on portages or do I want something that will survive an encounter with a rock on a river? Do I want a solo or a tandem boat?

The more I look at these options, the better my old canoe looks. I know every dent and scratch on its hull and there is a story behind every crease and nick. Yes, I would like a new boat customized for my next trip, but my old canoe does pretty well for most of my canoeing. I guess, for now, I can be satisfied with what I have.

Paul said we should be content whatever our circumstances. Regardless of whether we live, suffer or die we should be satisfied because we know that we exist in the love of Christ. We often lose sight of this ultimate victory and we worry about how we will handle problems instead of looking to Christ for strength. We want the newer, better, bigger version of whatever we have and forget that Christ's provision is enough.

What satisfies you? Are you satisfied with what God has provided for you?

Backpacking Blizzard

Scripture: Deuteronomy 1:20-45, Proverbs 3:5-6

I am well trained as a backpacker. I took college backpacking classes, planned and led backpacking trips and even worked at an adventure camp taking youth on backpacking, biking, climbing and rafting trips. So when it comes to the out-of-doors, I consider myself an able planner. I know the clothing to bring for each season and what clothing to avoid.

I was looking forward to a March backpacking trip in the mountains. I had hiked the Mt. Rogers area in Virginia during a previous summer and was anticipating returning to that area. The weather was fairly warm as I packed. So into my pack went two pairs of polypropylene, one pair of fleece pants and jacket, one lightweight rain coat, one pair of glove liners and on a whim, a pair of fleece mittens. A friend heard a weather report that predicted snow in the mountains. But I thought I knew best. After all, I was the backpacker.

As I drove toward the mountains, I began to see snowflakes. It snowed that evening as we set up camp. The next morning it warmed a little and drizzled as we ate breakfast and broke camp. My glove liners became a bit wet in the rain, so I got out my mittens.

We began hiking uphill. The higher we went, the more snow we saw. My wet fingers progressed from cold to frozen as we gained elevation and snow fell on us. I finally borrowed a pair of wool mittens. These also became wet and cold. I wore my lightweight rain coat and nylon pants over layers because that was all I brought. I wished that I had listened to my friend and brought my Gore-Tex jacket, rain pants and more layers.

When we finally set up camp, I was colder and more miserable than I ever been before. I crawled into the tent to get warm and put on my one dry fleece outfit.

To make the weather even more challenging, it warmed up just enough for the snow on the pines above our tent to begin to melt and pour down upon us. After cooking dinner outside in the cold air, I was ready to crawl back into the tent. That night the temperature dropped and the snow and water froze into icy patches around our campsite. I was now ready to go home where it was warm and dry!

That backpacking experience reminds me of the journey of the Israelites. God miraculously led them out of Egypt but they bitterly complained again and again. When they were about to enter their promised land, they did not listen to Moses who told them that God would give the land into their hands. They finally repented, but it was too late. An 11-day journey turned into four decades of wandering because they did not listen. Obeying God can prevent a variety of miserable situations in our lives.

Are you listening to God's voice? What has He been telling you lately?

Going Home

Scripture: Matthew 5:13-16

On outdoor trips, I tend to be goal-oriented. Each day my mind is set to work toward a specific objective. It may be a particular place to stop for lunch, a certain number of miles to accomplish by mid-afternoon or that night's campsite. Each of these goals are intermediate goals on my way to the ultimate goal: the end of the trip. This goal-oriented approach may be a reflection of my years in the workforce and I carry this business approach into my outdoor leisure activities.

Often in pursuit of these targets, I put my head down and I may miss the sights of the area I am traveling through. The sights and sounds around me are camouflaged by my need to get somewhere or accomplish a task. There may be a deer in the brush or a loon fishing in the lake, but in the pursuit of my daily goals I miss the beauty that surrounds me.

I usually think the trip is over when I get to the canoe take-out point, the trailhead or the car and prepare to go home. A better attitude would be that the trip home is the real beginning of the trip.

I participate in wilderness trips to enjoy the beauty of God's creation and to "recharge my batteries" for the time I must spend back at home and work. I need the change of pace and focus that I get in the wilderness. I need to be still and hear God speak to me. I need to commune with God in His creation. By recharging my batteries, I am refreshed and, in essence, a stronger "light" when I get home.

Jesus said, "You are the light of the world." If we are able to recharge by spending time in the wilderness and then do not return home to shine, we are hiding our light. I do not think that I will avoid aiming toward goals on my trips, but I will concentrate on expanding these goals to enjoy nature more. I will not let my goals get in the way of enjoying my trip and I will make it a point to shine to the world I live in when I return home.

Have you recharged your batteries lately? Are you a shining light in a dark world?

The Hill

Scripture: Philippians 4:11-13

When we left Canton that March morning, it was partly cloudy. By afternoon it had warmed up to the mid-60's. It started raining at the trailhead that evening and became cooler. On the second day it stopped raining, stayed cool and eventually started snowing in mid afternoon. By evening we were blindly trudging up a steep hill in the dark in several inches of snow with more rapidly falling. The temperature was dropping, it was late and the students were miserable. This was the first week-long backpacking trip for most of the group. The weather was worse than we had anticipated.

The leaders spread out among the small groups of students working on the grueling climb. Dave was farthest up the hill with the two fastest students. Eric was just ahead with three students and Chris and I were with Sue. We were all slipping and sliding, at times losing more than we gained on the slippery ground.

Chris and I walked on either side of Sue in case we needed to provide support. We encouraged her as she struggled up the steep incline, but we let her do her own work. Tears of frustration streamed down her cheeks in the snowy night.

By the time we reached the top, the lead groups had the tents set up and were starting to prepare supper. Sue remained quiet and thoughtful the rest of the evening. We finished the week with many changes in our plans due to the unexpected weather and cold temperatures.

In the summary papers the participants wrote about their experience, Sue wrote most about the "hill." She confessed to coming to the end or her resources. She had nothing left to get her up the hill and then through God she found more energy and determination than she ever knew she had. She explained that she used up all of this second energy source at which time God provided a third source.

Sue learned more about herself and God in that one week than in all her previous years. God provides what we need when we need it, if we are surrendered and dependent on Him as our source of strength. Sue graduated from college two months later, changing her career to serve God in ministry rather than teach school.

Have you pushed beyond your limits? What did you find? Do you trust God to provide?

God Saw That It Was Good

Scripture: Genesis 1:1-25

Coast redwoods (Sequoia sempervirens) grow to be over 350 feet tall. This compares to a 35 story building or longer than a football field. These massive trees are the tallest living things on earth. Their distinctive reddish color gives them their name. I was fortunate enough to live among these giants in northern California for several years. I will forever be awed by their size and beauty.

I wonder what God was thinking as He created the earth, light and dark, plants and animals. We have huge trees and microscopic algae, tall animals and tiny insects. It seems He planned everything as He fit nature's cycles together. Only He could have thought to have oxygen as the waste product of a plant's photosynthesis be the very thing that animals need to breathe. We do know that as each day's creation was completed, "God saw that it was good." The earth and all that was in it was brand new. There was no garbage, no pollution and life was sustainable.

I wonder what God thinks as He looks upon His creation today. We have polluted, destroyed, endangered and exploited the environment He so lovingly created. A recent television commercial showed a climber ascending stacked automobiles at a junkyard and a family camping in a parking lot. These ads show that we need to take care of our environment before there are no natural places left.

Why have we become so complacent about the environment that God created? Our trees are cut, forests mined and arctic drilled to satisfy our lust for things. Plant and animal species become extinct as we destroy the rain forest, pollute our air and water and develop more and more land area.

Our landfills quickly fill as it is estimated that each person throws away an average of 4½ pounds of garbage per day. Much of our garbage could be recycled, but as a nation we do not care enough about our planet and resources to do something that is inconvenient or takes a little more time.

So do we just give up on this monumental task of protecting our environment and wilderness areas? No! We need to teach others and set an example by recycling, reusing and conserving the wilderness. In natural environments, we dispose of our waste properly and hike and camp carefully to not leave traces of our presence. We leave natural items as we found them and respect wildlife and their habitat as we would expect our own homes to be respected by visitors. We must treat God's natural creation with the utmost of respect whether we are in the wild or at home.

Can others tell that you love Jesus by how you treat His creation?

Companions

Scripture: Matthew 28:16-20, Romans 1:19-20

I seldom go into the wilderness alone. Many times I take Scouts or other groups of people learning about the outdoors with me. Other times I take my family or a few close friends.

Although I would enjoy solo trips, I like having companions along. One reason for not taking solo trips is that the margin of safety is increased by having others with me. Should there be an accident, there will be other people to assist with the incident.

Safety is not the only reason for taking others on. My primary reason for having companions on outdoor trips is the wilderness experience is something that I want to share with as many people as possible. There are skills learned in the woods that can be applied throughout life. Leadership and self-sufficiency are easily taught in outdoor classrooms. Friendships are strengthened and new experiences bond people together.

What keeps calling me back to the wilderness is the beauty of God's creation. In Romans, Paul says that God's nature is apparent from what He has created. I cannot see wildlife, hear the birds or enjoy a panoramic view without feeling close to God. I understand Paul's words when I see God in the details of the leaves and storms.

By taking people into the wilderness I believe that I am helping fulfill the great commission: to go and make disciples throughout the earth. The outdoor experience allows people to encounter God through nature. Once they have seen God at work, they are more receptive to learn the Gospel message. When you choose companions on your next trip, consider choosing people who may not have previously experienced God. Your trip may make an eternal difference in their lives.

Are you sharing the beauty of God's creation with others? Who will your companions be on your next wilderness trip and for eternity?

Bad Maps

Scripture: John 14:1-7

Part of the preparation for any trip is to examine maps of the route. They are used to select your route, to determine where to camp, to identify water sources and possibly to find easy ways home if you need to return early or have an accident. Maps let you know what geographic conditions to expect. But what happens if the maps are wrong?

The Missinaibi River flows northeast into James Bay in Ontario. There is little access once you launch from Mattice until you reach the railroad 165 miles later. The remoteness makes this river an exciting wilderness trip.

The most famous terrain feature on this section of the river is Thunderhouse Falls where the river flows over the granite in the Canadian Shield into the Hudson Bay lowlands. This waterfall is really three falls with the river narrowing from several hundred yards wide to little more than a canoe length wide. The falls earned the name Thunderhouse because of the noise of its cascade and the vibrations it creates in the surrounding rocks.

Years ago, the Canadian government printed the topographical map for the region with a portage around the falls placed on river right, just above the falls. The actual portage was on the left side of the river and a distance before the falls. One group of canoeists did their preparation and used the map to plan their route. They planned to minimize their portage by taking this trail that was close to the falls. Unfortunately, they had the wrong information. The map was wrong. As a result of being on the wrong side of the river near the falls, one canoe was swept over the falls and two canoeists died.

What about in life? What maps do you use? Jesus said, "I am the way, the truth, and the life. No one comes to the Father except through Me". Without Jesus, reconciliation with God is impossible. The are no other routes to eternal life.

There are people who sincerely believe that they are following a good map for their lives. But, without putting their trust in Jesus as their Savior, they are following a bad map.

Have you made the commitment to Jesus which puts you on the right route for an eternal relationship with Him? Do you have friends who are sincere in their beliefs but do not know Christ? Are you willing to watch them flow over the falls when you can give them the right map?

Trust

Scripture: John 17:6-18, Psalm 19:5-7

Sam trusted me. We were rappelling down a 60-foot cliff. I was belaying at the bottom of the cliff. From this position it was my responsibility to stop the rappeller's descent if he or she encountered problems. Pulling on the rope would increase the friction on the figure-eight attached to the rappeller's harness and stop him from descending.

Sam had rappelled Australian style previously and wanted to try it again. In an Australian rappel the person descends the cliff head first. The previous time, someone else attached the system to his harness for him. Sam believed he knew how to do the setup and attachment. He attached the figure-eight with the rope to the back of his harness and was ready to go.

As soon as Sam stepped off the top of the cliff, it became obvious that the setup was wrong. There was not enough friction to slow him so he was very rapidly dropping toward the ground. With the setup wrong, I could not slow him down by pulling on the rope. My response was to run away from the face of the cliff pulling the rope out with me until there was enough distance to turn his straight drop into a diagonal slide. I was then able to slow his rush to the ground and use my body as a block at the end of his slide. We picked ourselves off the ground with no more problems than dust from the fall and a few bruises.

Sam took a chance, but had faith in me as a belayer. He was willing to trust his life to me. This was not necessarily wise on his part, since I was not able to control the setup that he had made. Fortunately we do not have to worry about the setups in our lives. God has made the perfect setup in the sacrifice of Jesus for our sins. In the Scripture,

Jesus prays for His disciples. He was nearly finished with his time with them and was trusting God for His disciples' future care. If Jesus trusts God for His disciples' care, can we do less than that?

Sam trusted me, a man. Do you trust God, the creator of the universe with the setup of your life? Where does your faith lie?

Learning from the Past

Scripture: Proverbs 1:1-19

After each of my outdoor trips, I write a summary of the experience. I make general notes about where I went and the date. I jot down items that I took that were useful or other items that I wished I had brought with me. The most important thing I do is make a list of new things that I learned. When I am packing for future trips, I look at my notes and remember the lessons and what gear would be most appropriate for the type of trip. These notes are probably the most important aspect of my trip. They help me remember what I did right, but I also learn from my mistakes.

On my very first backpacking trip, I learned a lesson about rain gear. I brought a yellow rubber raincoat. I am not sure if I was wetter from the rain or from my sweating inside the raincoat. I also brought a cotton flannel shirt that was soaked with sweat and left me chilled when we set up camp. Breathable raincoats are worth the price and I learned not to wear cotton when it is cool and raining.

During a winter trip, I learned that extra layers are worth the weight in my pack and I should expect worse weather at higher elevations. I learned the hard way that sport top water bottles are not very functional below freezing temperatures because you cannot drink out of them when water freezes in the top unless you store them upside down so the ice forms on the bottom. And the one trip I did not take a first-aid kit was the trip that I needed the ibuprofen the most, so I should always be prepared with it.

I also learn new things from camping with different groups of people. On one trip, I learned natural alternatives to toilet paper (rhododendron leaves work really well!). On another, I learned to eat with a bandana on my lap to catch crumbs and other food particles. I have also learned that I can swallow my toothpaste to keep it from polluting the environment and antibacterial hand cleaner helps when there are no hand-washing facilities.

In 1 Kings, Solomon asked God for wisdom. God rewarded Solomon with knowledge of a wide variety of topics, including plants and animals. He wrote and spoke thousands of proverbs that we still gain wisdom from today. Solomon's proverbs tell us that "the fear of the Lord is the beginning of knowledge".

Solomon later began to depend on himself and satisfy his fleshly desires. The wisest man ever, failed to remember the author of his wisdom and it became his downfall. Let us glean wisdom from Solomon's many proverbs. Let us also learn vicariously from Solomon's actions. We are not doomed to repeat history. God has given us a written record of His word so that we can learn from the successes and failures of past generations.

Have you learned from any mistakes lately? What wisdom are you gleaning from God's word?

The Things We Take for Granted

Scripture: Philippians 4:11-13, Joshua 1:2-9

Sinks with running water and flushable toilets are common household items in North America. I would venture a guess that most of us take these things for granted. We are so used to having them, that we do not think about using them until we go to the woods and these conveniences are no longer available. I remember that going to the bathroom was one of the most difficult parts of my first backpacking trip.

When we go backpacking or venture out in a canoe, there are many things that we leave behind like comfortable beds, microwaves and dishwashers. Things we expect to have in civilized life, are not available in the woods. Many tasks in the wilderness become more difficult, like opening a can or cooking a meal or even going to bed. You must set up a tent or tarp and get out a sleeping mat and your sleeping bag.

I think back to the pioneer days in America. Many people think those must have been the "good old days." Life was simple then. But was it really? Living was on a more subsistence level: if you needed it you grew it or made it or did without it. A trip to the "local" store may have taken a day (or more) on horseback. You sewed your own clothes, made your own soap, smoked your own meat, canned your own vegetables, even built your own home. Most of these are tasks that we take for granted in our current age. We usually buy all of these items pre-made.

There are many other things that we tend to take for granted: eyesight, hearing, even the abilities to walk and talk or smell and taste. We do not realize how important these are to us, until one of them is altered or impaired.

One adage says that there are lots of things we want when we are well, but the only thing we want when we are sick is to be well again.

The Israelites took God for granted again and again. In their journey to the promised land, they complained about water and food and then they made an idol while Moses was on the mountain receiving the ten commandments. They trusted God when times were good, but then tended to take matters into their own hands.

I wonder if that is not a comparison to our relationship with Jesus. When things are going well and we have our conveniences, we are more likely to take Him for granted. But when times are tough and our health is poor or finances uncertain, we either strike out on our own or begin to pray in earnest. Like Paul in Philippians 4:11-13, let us learn to depend on God in all circumstances, meditating on His word and observing His commands.

What things in your life are you taking for granted? Do you take Jesus for granted? His provision? Promises? Presence?

How Was Your Trip?

Scripture: Hebrews 11:1

I went backpacking this past weekend. It was a great spring weekend and we were on one of my favorite local trails. Since returning from the hike, most of the people who knew what I intended to do over the weekend asked me about my trip.

In some ways I find this amusing. I cannot remember an outdoor trip that I have not enjoyed. Of course, there are trips when problems occur with the weather (thunderstorms, wind, cold and snow) or we have an accident. But somehow these problems never seem important, especially in retrospect. When I go caving, I know that when I emerge, I will be bumped and bruised and have very sore shins. This does not diminish my anticipation of the next caving trip.

This experience of past great trips leads me to look forward to my next trip. I am currently anticipating a trip to Philmont Scout Ranch. I was there as a boy 35 years ago. That experience left me with the goal of returning to experience it again. A funny thing about this next trip is that I know Philmont has changed since I was a boy. The trails will be harder for me at this age than they were as a youth. Nonetheless, I look forward to the trip with greater anticipation than my first trip there.

Is faith like our outdoor trips? The writer of Hebrews describes faith as "being sure of what we hope for, being convinced of what we do not see." Just as weather and accidents are part of our outdoor trips, our lives also will have problems. But looking back, we can be confident that God was with us and blessed us in each season of our lives.

When we plan our next trip, we are sure that it will be a great experience, that we will thoroughly enjoy it. Our faith in God should be not just similar, but more certain. Looking forward, we can be sure that not only has God been with us in the past, but He will continue to be with us in all that we do. Anticipating our ultimate trip to spend eternity with Him, we can be certain of this future.

Do you anticipate your time spent with God?

Rock Praise

Scripture: Psalm 150

Fall colors ensconced the mountains of West Virginia. Dan and I cupped our hands around steaming mugs of hot drinks and bowls of oatmeal on the cool October morning. We sorted and packed our climbing gear and began the hike to the mountain base. It was a magnificent morning and we were excited about the coming day of climbing and its challenging opportunities. The anticipation brought praise to our hearts.

"Praise the Lord. Praise God in his sanctuary; praise him in his mighty heavens." (Psalm 150:1)

As we approached the rocks, the sun crept above a distant crest. The warmth of the sun allowed us to remove the heavy jackets we had needed earlier. We set up our first, easy climb on the east side of a ridge to catch the morning sun rays, which felt wonderful on our necks and arms. Our muscles limbered up with the warmth of the sun and exercise. We felt great and were energized for our day's plans.

"Know that the LORD is God. It is he who made us, and we are his; we are his people, the sheep of his pasture..."(Psalm 100:3)

The sky was bright blue with a few small white clouds casting floating shadows on a deep, golden-hued, sun-draped landscape. I was on a corner belaying Dan on a breath-taking climb. As I felt the change in pressure on the rope and listened for his calls I watched the valley below me. Occasionally a gust of wind would hit the trees and a cloud of yellow, burgundy, orange and brown leaves would spin into the air like a blizzard, spread out and slowly settle back toward earth. It was like silent fireworks.

"The earth is the Lord's and everything in it, the world, and all who live in it" (Psalm 24:1)

I felt contentment in my life. I do not feel that often enough. The combination of God's creation, good fellowship and a physical workout all came together to make it an excellent time. We talked little, because conversation interfered with the joy of the day. We had apples, cheese and hard rolls in our pack for lunch. The water in my bottle tasted sweet. Life was grand.

"For you make me glad by your deeds, O Lord; I sing for joy at the works of your hands. How great are your works, O Lord, how profound your thoughts!" (Psalm 92:4,5)

As long shadows descended on us we rappelled to the ground and hiked back to our campsite. We were weary, but happy. There was a slight fatigue and soreness that comes from an enjoyable workout. We had communed with the Lord in His domain. We sat around our fire that evening, reliving the day's events. We were thankful.

"Praise the Lord, O my soul; all my inmost being, praise his holy name. Praise the Lord, O my soul, and forget not all his benefits...who satisfies your desires with good things so that your youth is renewed like the eagle's."(Psalm 103:1,2,5)

Winter Trip

Scripture: Hebrews 13:16

It was the end of January. The winter had been cold and snowy, dipping to 21 degrees below zero on one occasion. My sons, Joshua and Joel and I had been planning a winter backpacking trip for several weeks for some private time together.

Four students I was working with at the university heard me mention the trip and begged to go along. I asked another leader to join us and take some responsibility for the students so I could still have some time with my sons.

After hiking to an overlook the first night, we camped in about 10 inches of snow. In the morning we awoke to two additional inches. Another tent had also joined us over the night, so three additional young men asked to join us for the day's hike.

It became a fantastic day as we hiked through a foot of snow on the trail. Late in the afternoon the sun broke through the clouds, casting long shadows from the trees across our path. Everyone stayed warm in the upper 20 degree temperature. The scenery was extraordinary with snow covering all of the landscape in a clean, white blanket that muffled sounds. There was a sense of awe among the group. Everyone talked in quiet tones rather than shouts and loud laughs.

I stayed at the back of the group with my sons as we hiked. We had a great time of talking and sharing while on the trail, yet we enjoyed the company of the others at lunch and around the campfire that evening. What was to be a private trip became more enjoyable because we chose to share it with others, some of whom we did not even know.

For years afterward, my sons would comment that this trip was one of their most enjoyable times of backpacking because of the beauty of the scenery and the enjoyment of sharing our "private" world with others.

Are you willing to be flexible and share your trips and your life with others? Do you share God?

Skunk

Scripture: John 3:1-6, Jonah 2:1-10

I remember, as a young boy, hiking with a group of friends in the woods around Leesville Lake on an overcast, damp, fall afternoon. Our tents were set up and our gear unloaded, so we explored the surrounding area. Traipsing through the woods, we saw a skunk. It waddled up a hill through the trees at a speed that surprised me. I did not believe a skunk could move that fast.

As typical kids, we began to chase after the skunk rather than choosing the wiser path of heading in the opposite direction. Fortunately, although we moved fast, we never succeeded in getting too close. We could keep up with the skunk, but were always about 20 yards behind.

We eventually quit our chase and started working our way back to camp. We discussed how brave we were in chasing a skunk and how fortunate the skunk was that we did not catch it.

We were caught up in a classic case of approach/avoidance. We wanted to catch the skunk, but we were concerned about the consequences if we got too close. We were curious, but also respectful. We would not admit that we held back in our chase, that we did not do our best to catch up to the skunk.

In a strange way, chasing the skunk parallels our pursuit of God. Often our relationship with God is one of approach/avoidance. We want to draw close, but we are wary of the consequences. We want to meet God personally, but we are concerned about the cost to us. We desire a relationship, but we want to avoid any changes to our lives.

Most of us are very familiar with this passage of Scripture from John. Nicodemus was truly trying to understand what Jesus was talking about. When Jesus told him that he must be born again from the Spirit, it challenged Nicodemus' sense of reality. Today we understand that Jesus was not talking about physical birth but of spiritual birth.

As we contemplate this spiritual birth, we begin thinking about the consequences. Will I be called to do something that I do not think I can do or do not want to do? It is wise to remember that "works for the good of those who love him, who have been called according to his purpose". He will not call us to do something that He will not give us the desire and ability to do.

Do you treat God like a skunk in your life? Do you draw near to Him and face the consequences or do you avoid Him? Do you worship God from afar, always keeping a safe distance or do you have a close personal relationship?

Wildflowers

Scripture: Genesis 1, Psalm 95:1-6

Do you look at the flowers when you are outside? There are certainly very pretty flowers grown in the gardens around our homes, but I think the ones that you find growing wild are prettier.

The next time you are outdoors, look at the wildflowers. Some are small, so take time to get down on their level and look at all of the patterns and colors built into a petal that may be no larger than a pinhead. Examine the intricacies of the jack-in-the-pulpit and the deep red of the trillium. This is one of the most magnificent colors in creation.

Consider the season when flowers bloom. The Creator made some of the forest flowers to bloom early in the spring before the canopy of leaves from the trees cut off the light needed for the plants to mature. Other flowers bloom very late in the year for similar reasons. Some flowers push up through the late spring snow, while others push up through the leaves of fall. The mountain flowers bloom early in the short summer season of the high altitudes while there is still moisture and the sun is less harsh.

Look at the creation story in Genesis. Wildflowers are such a small portion of God's creation. When you consider the creation of the universe, it is almost inconceivable that God would take the time to place a row of small dots on a flower petal. It is amazing that God would take the time to select the flaming red of the trillium. God is the God of details. He takes time for the details. Does that not also say that He takes time for us as individuals? He knows how we are created and the secrets of our hearts. He cares for the details in our lives.

Read Psalm 95 and think about the entire world that God has created. What is your response to His creation? Have you praised Him for the details? Have you given Him all the details of your life?

Note from the Authors

We hope that you have enjoyed these devotions and that reading them has touched you as much as writing them has touched us.

Please contact us with your feedback and experiences.

God bless you.

Amy, Jack, Jack and Larry

email: books@wildernessmonster.com

Notes

Notes

Notes

Notes

Notes

Notes

Notes

Notes

Notes

Notes

Notes

Notes

Notes

Notes

Notes

CPSIA information can be obtained
at www.ICGtesting.com
Printed in the USA
BVHW042020261118
534040BV00011B/786/P